CW00971609

AIRWISE

AIRWISE

The guide to free and discounted air travel

D. FARRY

Tynron Press, Scotland

© *Wanderscan Ltd., 1989*

This edition first published in 1990 by
Tynron Press
Stenhouse
Thornhill
Dumfriesshire DG3 4LD

ISBN 1-871948-97-5

All rights reserved

Important
The information contained in this guide has been published in good faith on the basis of information supplied and researched by the author. Air travel conditions and schemes may be altered, suspended or withdrawn at very short notice. No responsibility for any error or mispresentation is accepted and all liability for loss, disappointment, negligence or other damage caused by the reliance on the information contained in this guide, or in the event of the withdrawal, suspension or modification of any scheme, promotion or offer by any company, individual or firm mentioned, or in the event of the bankruptcy or liquidation of any company, individual or firm mentioned, or in the event of any company, individual or firm ceasing to trade, is hereby excluded.

Cover design by Beatrice Ling
Typeset by Linographic Services Pte Ltd
Printed in Singapore by General Printing Services Pte Ltd

CONTENTS

Dedicated to my wife Kath,
and family, Sinead, Gemma and Mick.
Special thanks to Joe Morgan
for the illustrations.
No thanks at all to those
engaged in the business
of providing and supplying air travel
whose obtuseness, over-regulation,
self-serving interests and
lack of service to the customer which
regretfully make such a guide as this
necessary.

FOREWORD

Airwise is a brand new concept in travel publications, enabling anyone to slash or completely eliminate the cost of air travel — so you can forget rising interest rates, the plummeting value of the pound and get away for far less than you think, using little known methods of air travel.

There are many travel guides available which give information on what to do or see when you arrive in a foreign country.

This manual is unique since it tells you *how to get there by the cheapest possible means.*

This guide has been written for both business and leisure use by the independent traveller — with the express aim of slashing the cost of scheduled air travel. Airlines are, by nature, unwilling to divulge their particular practice regarding ticketing, preferring to shroud this topic in a welter of detailed conditions, which only serve to confuse the traveller, with the express purpose of pushing one into a higher fare category than is absolutely necessary.

This attitude stems firstly from the desire of a country to protect its national carrier and secondly the problem of over-capacity on transatlantic routes. If an airline is flying a route with its planes only 50% full, then it makes sense (to the airline, not the passenger, that is) to charge as expensive a fare as possible, in order to maximise the income from that route.

A sane person might question this attitude and possibly ponder the unthinkable notion that a reduction in fares, a simplification of ticket conditions and the introduction of competition might just help to fill the empty seats and increase income at the same time.

Deregulation in the United States has helped to solve many of the problems still encountered in Europe and it is both in, and to, the United States that the greatest travel bargains are to be had.

The information contained within the book is concerned with scheduled flights only; it is *not* concerned with tickets obtained through bucket shops, where caution is advised, nor is it concerned with cheap charters which are often too inflexible to be seriously considered.

It is *not* associated in any way with timeshare or property bond inspection flights.

It is *not* concerned with offers giving "free" accommodation with flights *nor* promotions offering "free" air travel if hotel accommodation (with meals included) is booked.

There is no such thing in life as a free lunch!

Within these pages is the information you can use to fly free or at greatly reduced rates, e.g. Concorde to New York for about 20% of the standard fare, as often as you wish (the only restriction being the time you have at your disposal to take up the free and reduced rate fares available) and the further free and reduced rate allowances, which your flights will generate.

Freddie Laker once said, "After women, wine and horses, I can think of no more enjoyable or pleasurable way of spending large amounts of money quickly, than on airlines and air travel."

This guide is designed to give you the enjoyment and pleasure of air travel — without spending large amounts of money.

TICKETING

Reservations and ticketing are separate functions in airlines, the former being the intention to fly, the latter being allowed to board. This is an important distinction of use to the traveller.

Reservations

A reservation is the notification to an airline that one wishes to fly. It does not normally bind either the traveller nor the airline to take the particular flight booking nor does it normally entail any monetary loss to the traveller if he does not take up that booking. The advantage of this to the traveller is that several reservations can be made for flights to a particular destination if he is unsure which flight he wishes to catch, because of time etc., safe in the knowledge that he can get on one of them. Secondly, there is the distinct possibility that he can fly at a reduced stand-by rate, if the reservations have been made under several different names. Obviously, this does *not* apply to pre-paid budget tickets where the ticket is lost if the passenger does not show. Under IATA (International Air Traffic Association) rules, holders of full-fare tickets can change flight timings, airlines, or even obtain refunds, without undue difficulty. What this means is that an airline which had previously thought it had a particular flight fully booked can suddenly find that it has empty seats, which if remaining unsold, can lead to a large loss of revenue. To overcome this problem, airlines will overbook flights, since it is known from previous experience, that in addition to the above circumstances, there will be other reasons for previously booked passengers not turning up for their flights (e.g. delayed connections, illness, etc.).

Reservation Status

On airline tickets this is denoted in the status box by these codes: OK (Space confirmed); RQ (Space requested but not confirmed, or placed on waiting list); NS (Infant without any right to a seat); SA (Advance reservations not allowed, but boarding allowed, subject to space being available).

Overbooking and Compensation

When overbooking occurs, and more passengers with confirmed reservations than seats turn up for a particular flight, the excess passengers get "bumped". In Europe, bumping can either be up or down in class e.g. Economy to First Class or vice versa. In a common class flight, bumping is done in order of check-in. In the United Kingdom, if bumping occurs and the passenger is transferred to another flight which arrives at his destination more than four hours after the scheduled arrival time, he is entitled to receive compensation at the rate of 50% of the single leg fare for that destination.

In the United States, bumping is done on a volunteer basis. If insufficient volunteers come forward, then the airline can bump on a last check-in basis, as in Europe. For involuntary bumping, the American rules are, that if the passenger is unable to be rescheduled onto another flight due to arrive within four hours of his original flight, the airline must pay compensation at twice the cost of the ticket. In addition, the passenger gets to keep his ticket for later use. These are general guidelines only, some airlines will offer more, others less. In case of doubt, barter!

IATA Fares Make Up

Because of the international nature of the IATA membership, difficulties arise through currency differences. Since IATA fares for any destination can be bought in any country, savings can be made by exploiting this in a country where the currency is weak. IATA has attempted to overcome this problem by periodically issuing currency adjustment tables, tabulated in terms of FCUs (Fare Currency Units) to allow exchange rate conversion but these are well behind what is actually happening to a country's currency.

Maximising Currency Differences

Purchasing of tickets abroad may be done using currency, traveller's cheques or credit cards. In addition, MCOs (Miscellaneous Charges Orders) or a UATP card (Universal Air Travel Plan) may be used. Both of these are issued by the airlines, for purchase of air transportation and related items. The method of purchase to be used in maximising the currency advantage to the traveller, is dependent on what is happening to the currency of the particular foreign country in relation to the United Kingdom. If it is "softening" then credit cards should be considered, since the transaction will be converted into sterling at the rate ruling at the time of presentation. This may be some time distant, since overseas purchases, undertaken by credit card, can take up to three months to appear on a statement, and the sterling exchange rate could be very favourable to the cardholder. Conversely, currency or currency equivalents, such as MCOs should be used if the currency of the country in question is "strengthening" against sterling.

Cross-Border Ticketing

What has been written above refers to normal methods of using currency differences, and must *not* be confused with cross-border ticketing. Cross-border ticketing arises from a dual situation of fare anomalies and currency movements, which can best be explained in relation to transatlantic air fares, for higher priced tickets, such as Business or First Class. On high volume air routes, such as London — New York, the fare charged can be more expensive than from Athens — New York via London, by as much as 25–30%. Cross-border ticketing takes advantage of this anomaly by the issue of a ticket, for Athens — London — New York and return, when a direct London — New York and return ticket request is what is required. The Athens — London portion is simply discarded. This method of ticketing is used widely by discounted travel outlets because of its financial advantage to the traveller, but results in loss to the airlines.

Cross-border ticketing is not illegal, but it has to be stressed that IATA rules regarding flight coupons state that they must be used in sequence. This is designed to prevent the above situation, and the resultant loss to the airlines, from occurring. In the example above, if the airline discovered that the outward portion of the ticket (Athens — London sector) had not been used, while the traveller was in the United States, it *can* and almost certainly *will* refuse to honour the rest of the ticket, as it is entitled to do under IATA rules. The traveller will then have to purchase a one-way ticket from New York to London, in order to return home; and an expected financial gain will have turned into a heavy loss.

Fare Currency Units and Maximum Permitted Mileages

To attempt to overcome the difficulties in international ticketing, the Airline Passenger Tariff (issued by IATA to its members) therefore lists fares in terms of the above. This publication lists fares in both local currency and Fare Currency Units (FCUs). For an international ticket covering several stopover points, the FCUs are added up and then translated back into the currency of the country where the fare is being paid. Secondly, each route has a Maximum Permitted Mileage (MPM). What this means to the traveller is that, provided that the MPM for a particular route is not exceeded, any number of points in between the start and end of the journey can be visited, at no extra charge. This is because the agreed MPM for any particular route exceeds the actual mileage between the two points, by as much as 20–25%.

Free Stopover Points Using MPM

By making use of the MPM system for calculating the distance between two points, other additional points on the route can be visited, for the same fare than if the direct routing had been used. What this means to the traveller is best explained by the following examples.

Example 1:   London — Montreal direct route

The maximum permitted mileage for this route is 3,902 miles. But by making use of MPM, the following points can be included as stopovers, free of charge.

London — Manchester — Dublin — Glasgow — Montreal

On this indirect routing, the sum of the ticketed point mileage is only 3,484 miles which is 418 miles less than the MPM for the direct routing. Therefore no surcharge is made.

Example 2:   London — Toronto

Here the MPM for the direct route is 4,263 miles. But similarly, as in Example 1, Manchester, Dublin and Glasgow can be included, free of charge, since the sum of the ticketed point mileage for this routing is 3,773 miles, 490 miles less than the MPM.

Fare Construction Points

Using the Airline Passenger Tariff system, fares can be cut by up to about 25%, if a location, which is cheaper to fly to (but which the traveller has no intention of going to), is included in the fare construction, but *not* included in the writing of the ticket. This is "fictitious fare point ticketing". The reason for doing this is that the "fictitious fare point" used in constructing the fare, will be an unpopular point for travellers. (This is why a lower fare is offered.) Its inclusion in the fare build-up serves to establish a turnaround point. The use of this location as a "fictitious fare point" is indicated on airline tickets by the location being circled, to indicate that it is a turnaround point e.g. if Algiers was the fictitious fare point, then this would be circled on the ticket. It has to be pointed out, however, that this type of fare construction, under IATA rules, is not applicable to air travel undertaken wholly within Europe. To avail oneself of this facility for travel to the Mediterranean countries, one would have to make use of a North African point. A fare construction point often used in these circumstances is Algiers, since the

London — Algiers fare is cheaper than the fare from London to any European Mediterranean destination.

Miscellaneous Charges Orders

These are vouchers which can be purchased from any major airline denominated in the currency of the country where they have been bought, which can be used to purchase goods and services from any IATA airline. An MCO has a maximum value of $350 and is converted into the currency of the country where used at the prevailing exchange rate.

Why Purchase MCOs?

One reason for using an MCO is that because of currency fluctuations, the MCO, denominated in hard currency will purchase more "value", if used in a country where the currency is soft and declining in value, than if a ticket for that leg of the journey had been purchased in advance originally. Secondly, many countries require exit tickets to be produced upon entry to them, and the MCO is accepted by them as evidence of intended onward travel. This saves the difficulties of attempting to have a complicated ticket rewritten in a distant location, and therefore gives maximum flexibility. In addition to using MCOs for purchase of air transport, they may also be used for the following:
Car hire/rental, hotel accommodation, inclusive tours, upgrading Flight Class, deposits/down payments, Excess Baggage Charges or baggage shipped as cargo.

Open Jaw Ticketing

Open jaw ticketing is a return ticket written as follows:
Travel outward from A to point B
Travel inward from C to point A
The unflown sector B to C may be used in the calculation of the fare.

Round The World Ticketing

Round the world tickets are offered by partnerships of all the major airlines, and offer scope for considerable savings over direct fares, to particular destinations. The general conditions attaching to them are that there must be a minimum number of stopovers en route, and travel must be in a continuous global direction around the world. As an illustration of their use in cutting business travel costs, consider the case of a flight from London — Tokyo. The normal First Class fare for this route is £4,568, whereas the lowest round the world fare at the time of writing, ex-London which includes Tokyo in the itinerary is £895, a saving of £3,673 or 80% of the First Class direct fare. Round the world tickets are available from a number of airlines covering a set pattern of stopovers, or they can be written to the traveller's preferences. It is in the latter format where their use in cutting business travel costs can be maximised, when time is not at a premium and a number of foreign locations need to be visited. The route needs to be planned and finalised about two or three weeks before the expected departure date. However, if this is not possible, the ready-made round the world routings available from the airlines still offer considerable savings: the lowest ready-made including Tokyo in the itinerary is £1,445, saving £3,123 or 68% of the direct First Class fare.

CONTACT POINTS

Trailfinders, 42–48, Earls Court Road, London, W8 6EJ. Telephone 01-938 3366 (Longhaul), 01-937 5400 (USA/Europe), 01-938 3444 (1st/Business Class)

British Airways: A brochure listing routings, stopovers and the cost of round the world fares is available from any BA Sales Office.

FARES & TICKET TYPES

First (Code F): Stopovers allowed, no advance purchase requirement, no minimum stay, no altered booking charge, no cancellation charge.

Business (Code J/C): Conditions as above.

Economy (Code Y): Conditions as above.

Excursion (Code YE): Stopovers allowed, no advance purchase requirement, stay requirements are variable, no altered booking charge, no cancellation charge.

APEX (Code YAP): No stopovers allowed, advance purchase periods vary, charges made for altered bookings and cancellation.

PEX: No stopovers, minimum stay is three months, charges made for altered bookings and cancellations.

As a general rule of thumb, the price of a full Economy fare can be as little as 25% of the cost of the First Class fare but with little loss of benefits. A full Economy fare normally entitles the holder to make several stopovers along the way at no additional cost, provided the MPM is not exceeded

The posting of changed fares by airlines has been greatly simplified in the United Kingdom. The airline now has only to inform the Civil Aviation Authority (CAA) of its intention to charge a different fare, thirty days before introducing it.

If you are a frequent traveller then you are advised to take advantage of the special deals in "Bonus Travel" (e.g. 1,000 air miles credit is given when you use your Visa credit card for booking). Also, the information regarding traveller and passenger clubs in "Furthermore" could be of assistance. Infrequent travellers, where time and date of travel is not critical, should consider "Courier Services" where free flights and massive reductions on scheduled routes are available.

BONUS TRAVEL

Frequent flier programs started in the United States and Canada many years ago, firstly, as a way to attract customers to the airline in order to increase market share, and secondly to maintain customer loyalty, by offering regular fliers bonuses and incentives, based on the amount of individual or company expenditure or on miles flown with it. The programs have not been marketed in Europe to any great extent, until recently, for a number of reasons:

(a) Because of the limited amount of deregulation on European routes, carriers have tended to share revenue on routes under bilateral agreements and new competitors have been shut out of the market.

(b) Though multiple designation (allowing more than two airlines per route) is available, "fifth freedom" rights do not apply fully yet. However, moves to introduce these fully by 1992 are in train, due to strong pressure being put on national airlines and governments by the European Commissioners. "Fifth freedom" rights are when country A's airline picks up passengers in country B, and carries them to country C, in competition with carriers from countries B and C.

(c)   There has been little incentive for airlines to compete for business because most European airlines were state owned and resistant to consumer pressure. However, this has changed with the privatisation of British Airways and the aggressive push for business pursued by BA since.

(d)   There are possible tax problems in the United Kingdom for corporate travellers availing themselves of the programs, since the Inland Revenue may treat the awards received as compensation and thus liable to tax. The limited amount of freedom available under Common Market regulations to encourage an "open skies" policy allows new entrants to compete on certain high density routes, and an obvious way of establishing brand loyalty for newcomers is to introduce frequent flier programs in Europe. Despite the limitations, it is obvious that the widespread marketing of the programs in Europe will not be long delayed. In fact some of the major European airlines are already service partners in the American frequent flier programs. Although, initially, awards under the programs tended to offer the frequent traveller free further travel, the concepts have now been extended to other travel-related purchases, such as car rentals and hotel accommodation. The main benefits stemming from the various programs on offer are as follows:

    (i)   Free upgrades from one class to a higher class, once a minimum number of miles have been flown, e.g. Economy to Executive.

    (ii)   Free car rental, and choice of vehicle rented, from compact to luxury, depending on the miles travelled.

    (iii) Free or discounted hotel accommodation.

The major frequent flier programs are:
Pan Am Worldpass, American Airlines AAdvantage, TWA Frequent Flight Bonus, Aeroplan, United Airlines Mileage Plus. In Europe, British Airways Air Miles scheme.

Program Members & Benefits

American Airlines AAdvantage was the first travel awards scheme to be introduced. It is operated in conjunction with American Eagle, British Airways, Cathay Pacific, Qantas Airways and Singapore Airlines. For flights on these airlines to the United States, you earn mileage credit at the rate of 100% — Coach on Economy Class, 125% — Business, Club, Marco Polo Business Class, 150% — First Class or Concorde.

TWA Frequent Flight Bonus Program

The service partners in this program are: TWA and associated TWA companies, British Airways, Japan Air Lines, Piedmont Airlines, Hilton Hotels, Marriott Hotels, and Hertz Car Rental.

TWA offers a Platinum Points Program in conjunction with its Frequent Flier Program for transatlantic flights only. That is, in addition to the awards earned for being a frequent flier, extra benefits are earned through the Platinum Points Program (e.g. for each transatlantic segment, either 4 or 6 points are earned). These additional awards are a free companion ticket to any TWA destination in the United States/Caribbean for 20 points, two free First Class round trip tickets to any TWA domestic or international destination or free membership of the TWA Ambassador Club, worth $1,750, for 120 points.

Aeroplan

Members of this program include Air Canada, Air France, Air New Zealand, Lufthansa, Cathay Pacific, Hilton Hotels, CN Hotels, Budget, Avis and Hertz Car Rental.

The benefits from the programs, with membership costing about $25, can best be illustrated, by looking in depth at Aeroplan under the benefits available: Air Travel, Car Rental and Hotel Accommodation.

AIR TRAVEL

Qualifying Mileage	Benefits Available
8,000	Buy one North American Full Fare Economy ticket, and obtain a second ticket at 25% discount.
10,000	Upgrade from Full Fare Economy to Executive Class in North America.
30,000	One FREE North American Executive Class or Economy Class ticket.
40,000	Two FREE North American Economy Class tickets.
60,000	Two FREE North American First Class tickets.
100,000	Two FREE Economy Class tickets to Europe or the Caribbean.
120,000	Two FREE Economy Class tickets to Asia.
150,000	Two FREE First Class tickets to Europe or the Caribbean.
175,000	Two FREE First Class tickets to Asia.
250,000	Two FREE Economy Class Round the World tickets.

CAR RENTAL

Qualifying Mileage	Benefits Available
8,000/10,000	Rent for 3 days, pay for 2, third day FREE.
30,000	50% discount off 7 days economy car rental.
40,000	FREE 7 days economy car rental.
60,000	FREE 7 days compact car rental.
100/120,000	FREE 7 days full size car rental.
150/250,000	FREE 7 days luxury car rental.

HOTEL ACCOMMODATION

Qualifying Mileage	Benefits Available
8,000/10,000	Upgraded accommodation, at no extra charge.
30,000	30% off the published rate.
40,000	40% off the published rate.
60,000	FREE 3 consecutive nights.
100,000	FREE 5 consecutive nights.
120,000	FREE 6 consecutive nights.
150/250,000	FREE 7 consecutive nights.

Additional Mileage Credits Using Credit Cards

Mileage credits can be further boosted by using credit cards for the purchase of flight tickets and, indeed, any other goods. This is because the airlines running the programs also issue their own credit cards, in association with both Visa and Mastercard. These are similar in every respect to the regular versions of these cards, with one major exception — every time that they are used, mileage credits are gained, so that your frequent flier awards build up faster.

UNITED AIRLINES MILEAGE PLUS

This program issues a generic version of Mastercard.

PAN AM WORLDPASS, TWA FREQUENT FLIGHT BONUS PROGRAM

These programs issue generic versions of Visa. In the case of the TWA Visa card, on acceptance by the company, the following benefits are obtained:

(a)   A free upgrade certificate, which can be used to upgrade the ticket, from one class to a higher class.

(b)   The first time that the card is used to purchase a round trip ticket, an additional 1,000 bonus miles is given, provided that it is used within six months of receipt.

(c)   For continued membership, a $50 certificate, able to be used against any TWA ticket costing $300 or more, is given. Common to all cards is that for every purchase made using them, additional bonus miles are gained, at the rate of one mile for every dollar. This is a much superior benefit to the bonus earned on the British Airways Air Miles scheme using the Nat West Access (Mastercard) where 1 air mile is given for every $10 spent!

Using Courier Tickets with Frequent Flier Programs

"Courier Services" has details on how one is able to obtain free and reduced rate travel by acting as an air courier. For maximization of benefits, this should be combined with membership of a program. The following should also be borne in mind. In order to be able to avail oneself of the frequent flier awards mentioned one has to furnish the airlines with proof that travel has been made with them. This proof is either in the form of the used ticket stub, or a photocopy of it. (Some courier companies retain the ticket stubs; so you will have to obtain a photocopy of these stubs from them as it will assist in getting your awards faster.) If this is not possible, the flight destination and number, together with your name, as per the passenger list, should be forwarded, when you claim your award.

Applying for Membership of Frequent Flier Clubs

Applications for membership of the programs mentioned should be made to the following addresses:

PAN AM WORLDPASS
Pan Am WorldPass, Frequent Traveller System, Pan Am World Airways, Inc., P.O. Box 4080, Woburn, Maine, MA 0188 U.S.A.

TWA FREQUENT FLIGHT BONUS
Trans World Airlines, Inc., Frequent Flight Bonus, P.O. Box 767, Philadelphia, PA 19105 U.S.A.

AEROPLAN
Air Canada, Aeroplan, 1411, Fort Street, Montreal, Quebec, Canada, H3H 9Z9

UNITED AIRLINES MILEAGE PLUS
United Airlines Mileage Plus, United Airlines, Inc., P.O. Box 66100, Chicago, Illinois, IL 60666 U.S.A.

BRITISH AIRWAYS AIR MILES
Air Miles, Airlink House, Hazelwich Ave., Three Bridges, Crawley, West Sussex, RH10 1NP

AMERICAN AIRLINES AADVANTAGE
American Airlines, AAdvantage Membership Dept., P.O. Box 610943, Dallas/Fort Worth Airport, TX 75261-0943

Frequent Flier Programs

Air travel is a fast moving industry in every sense of the word and it is advisable to check with the airlines concerned what benefits are available from their programs, since these are liable to constant update and refinement.

In order to keep track of alterations and changes to frequent flier programs, there are two American publications which publish monthly updates on these. These are as shown below:
(a) *Business Flyer*. For information telephone 010-1-322-1238.
(b) *Frequent*. In addition to providing information you may also get a U.S. address for enrolment through this publication if this is required by the program. Telephone 010-1-597-8889

Frequent flier awards may be purchased or exchanged by using specialist frequent flier coupon brokers Some airlines allow awards to be transferred. Others do not; and this should be queried with the broker, prior to any transaction being finalised.

FREQUENT FLIER AWARD BROKERS
Airline Coupon Co.   Tel. 010-1-354-4489
International Air Coupon Exchange   Tel. 010-1-558-0053

GROUP TRAVEL

This guide is written for the independent traveller, that is, someone who:
(a) Does not wish to be packaged by a travel company, which may suit the company, and not the traveller.
(b) Seeks the best value for money possible but not necessarily the cheapest product available.
(c) Requires that the travel trade suits them, and not vice versa.

Such sentiments are becoming expressed more profoundly in the package holiday trade echoing the disenchantment of the general public to the goods on offer and extend also to the scheduled airline services, on which this guide concentrates. All the major airlines have responded to this emergent market preference by setting up specialist group travel sales sections to offer the independent traveller or group, the means to put their own package together.

These specialist sections deal with the following:
(a) Common interest groups

(b)   Convention or conference delegates
(c)   Incentive travel

The definition of a group varies between airlines. Size can vary from 10 to 20 or more. Generally, depending on the group size, in addition to special low fares, there will be at least one free ticket per group.

As an indication of the type of service given by the group sales departments of airlines, the TWA Group Travel Service offers the following services to group organisers:
(a)   TWA defines a group as consisting of 10 people or more.
(b)   Special low rate fares are available.
(c)   In addition to allocating seats, en bloc boarding passes are issued in advance with the tickets to avoid boarding delays.
(d)   Special group check-in areas are used and exclusive group travel lounges are also available at major airports.
(e)   Personalised publicity material can be provided for the group.
(f)   Finally hotel, car and coach hire can also be arranged at favourable rates.

This is the type of arrangement which any group organiser can expect from the group sales department of any of the major airlines.

In respect of the discounts given to groups, policy varies between airlines. Some airlines quote special fares; others will give discounts off their normal cheapest fare. These vary according to destination and season. Some indication of the deals on offer can be judged from the examples below:

CYPRUS AIRWAYS For a minimum group size of 20 people, there are discounts available, ranging between 44–47% off the normal excursion fare with a free ticket per group of 40 people.

VIRGIN ATLANTIC AIRWAYS For a group size of 20 people or more, discounts of 15%–20% are available off the normal Economy fare. This equates to either 3 or 4 free Economy tickets.

Apart from group fares or discounts available as shown, airlines give across-the-board discounts to other groups of travellers. Apart from groups wishing to be organised on a basis such as special interest, convention or conference and for whom the "tailored arrangements" mentioned previously apply, further segmentation takes place on other groups who can be classified as shown below by:
(a)   Age
(b)   Status
(c)   Occupation

No common policy exists for these particular types but the type of offer available will normally be a substantial discount off the normal fare subject to certain conditions. The type of deal which can be expected in respect of these types of travellers is shown below in an easy-to-read table format.

Category	Discount off normal fare %	Conditions to be observed
AGE		
Infant	90	Under 2 years
Child	50	Under 12 years.
Youth	25	Over 12 BUT under 22 years.
Student	55	Between 22 and 28 years.
OCCUPATION		
A/line staff	90	
Travel Agent	75	On IATA airlines
Staff (IATA)	FREE	a. On new pathfinder routes.

		b. On shuttles if not required for fare-paying passengers
Ship crews	40	

STATUS

First Class	50	Discount applies to accompanying spouse round-trip fare.
Club		
Economy		

In addition special offers are also available as shown below.

First Class	FREE	Virgin Atlantic offers FREE Economy tickets with every First Class ticket.
Entertainer	FREE	If you are a performer, artiste or magician etc. who would be willing to stand in the aisles of the plane and entertain fellow passengers on the journey Virgin may offer you FREE travel.
Pensioners	10	Discount off ALL fares including discounted fares, if aged 65 plus with United Airlines "Silver Wings Plus".

For further information on the fares, services and airlines mentioned in this brief rundown please contact the following:

TRANS WORLD AIRLINES, INC., Group Travel Service, 200, Piccadilly, London, W1V 0DH 01-439 5956

CYPRUS AIRWAYS LTD., Euston Centre, 29–31, Hampstead Rd., London, NW1 3JA 01-388 7981

VIRGIN ATLANTIC LTD., Ashdown House, High St., Crawley, West Sussex, RH10 1DQ 0293-562345/38222 0293-543843 Gatwick Airport

UNITED AIRLINES, INC., "Silver Wings Plus", P.O. Box 66100, Chicago, Illinois, IL 60666 USA

Finally, it is considered appropriate here to point out that airline policies and rebate schemes are likely to change or be altered, often at very short notice and this should always be borne in mind by prospective organisers who are warned to check with the airline first that the particular scheme is still in effect, prior to making any firm arrangements.

OFFICIAL AID

If you are in business or run your own business as a growing number of people do, then the Government will help you to combine business with pleasure by paying you grants towards travel costs abroad. Under the export initiative schemes, the Department of Trade & Industry will pay grants towards travel costs of up to £900 per person, for a group of up to four people, participating in an approved trade mission abroad. The export schemes divide into two categories:

(a)   Outward Missions
(b)   Trade Fairs

Outward Missions

The purpose of this scheme is to encourage businessmen to visit overseas markets to explore possible opportunities and assess prospects for their goods and services abroad. In order to make use of this opportunity the mission must be organised by a trade association, chamber of commerce or other such body, that will act as sponsor. The role of the sponsor is to:

(1) Organise the mission.
(2) Report to the British Overseas Trade Board (BOTB) on the mission.
(3) Submit claims for travel grants.
(4) Provide a co-ordinator for participants.
(5) Confirm attendance of participants.

Participants need to:
(1) Apply through the sponsor for participation.
(2) Be competent to supply the product or service offered.
(3) Establish sales links in/to the country visited, if needed.
(4) Attend any sponsor's briefing meetings.
(5) Provide evidence of travel expenditure when submitting claim.

Trade Fairs

The purpose of trade fairs is to bring groups of British business-men into personal contact with overseas buyers at exhibitions and fairs overseas organised by the BOTB. Participants are required to take or share a stand, staff it during the duration of the fair, and provide such exhibits of products or services as are required.

Travel Grants Available

The financial assistance available is similar under both schemes, with the exception that the Outward Mission scheme assistance is not available for participation in events in the USA, Canada, South Africa and Western Europe (except for Spain, Portugal, Iceland and Finland).

Level of Financial Assistance Available

The level of financial assistance available for various countries falls within the bands below. The amount of grant stated is per person for groups of up to four people and at 50% of the amount for additional participants.

Amount of travel grant £	Countries
100–200	Algeria, Czechoslovakia, Finland, Hungary, East Germany, Israel, Iceland, Malta, Poland, Morocco, Portugal, Spain, Yugoslavia, Tunisia.
201–300	Bulgaria, Canada, Cyprus, Egypt, Greece, USSR, United States, Jordan, Romania, Syria, Turkey.
301–400	Bahamas, Bahrain, Bangladesh, Barbados, Cuba, Ethiopia, India, Kenya, Kuwait, Lesotho, Oman, Mexico, Nepal, Nigeria, Pakistan, Puerto Rico, Qatar, Saudi Arabia, Senegal, Sudan, United Arab Emirates, Trinidad, Yemen (North & South).
401–500	Angola, Botswana, Brunei, Cameroun, Gambia, El Salvador, Ghana, Dominican Republic, Guyana, Haiti, Ivory Coast, Jamaica, Liberia, Panama, Mongolia, Sierra Leone, Somalia, Sri Lanka, South Africa, Surinam, Swaziland, Tanzania, Togo, Uganda, Zaire, Zambia.
501–600	Burma, Brazil, China, Colombia,

	Ecuador, Gabon, Guatamala, Honduras, Hong Kong, Laos, Malawi, Mozambique, Nicaragua, Venezuela, Zimbabwe.
601–700	Bolivia, Malaysia, Mauritius, Paraguay, Peru, Philippines, Singapore, Uruguay, Vietnam.
701–800	Australia, Chile, Indonesia, Japan, Korea.
801–900	Fiji, New Zealand

The above rates apply to a visit to *one* country only. If more than one country is visited on an Outward Mission lasting more than 10 days, special rates apply and examples of these special rates are given below.

Amount of travel grant	Group of countries visited
£800	Japan, Korea, Hong Kong and Singapore.
£915	Australia and New Zealand.

FURTHER INFORMATION

Further information on the schemes and assistance available can be obtained from the following sources:

Outward Missions

Fairs & Promotions Branch, British Overseas Trade Board, Dean Bradley House, 52, Horseferry Road, London, SW1P 2AG Tel. 01-212 0093/6277

Outward Missions & Trade Fairs

BOTB Regional Offices
SOUTH EAST Ebury Bridge House, Ebury Bridge Road, London, SWIW 8QD Tel. 01-730 9678

WEST MIDLANDS Ladywood House, Stephenson Street, Birmingham, B2 4DT Tel. 021-632 4111
EAST MIDLANDS Severns House, 20, Middle Pavement, Nottingham, NG1 7DW Tel. 0602 506181
NORTH WEST Sunley Tower, Piccadilly Plaza, Manchester, M1 4BA Tel. 061-236 2171
NORTH EAST Stanegate House, 2, Groat Market, Newcastle, NE1 1YN Tel. 091-232 4722
SOUTH WEST The Pithay, Bristol, BS1 2PB Tel. 0272 272666
YORKSHIRE & HUMBERSIDE Priestley House, Park Row, Leeds, LS1 5LF Tel. 0532 443171

In addition the following offices also act as contact points for the BOTB.

WALES Welsh Office, Industry Dept., New Crown Building, Cathays Park, Cardiff, CF1 3NQ Tel. 0222 825097
SCOTLAND Export Office, Industry Dept., Alhambra House, 45, Waterloo St., Glasgow, G2 6AT Tel. 041 248 2855
N. IRELAND IDB Northern Ireland, IDB House, 64, Chicester St., Belfast, BT1 4JX Tel. 0232 233233

Other Government Departmental Assistance

If you are not in business or running your own business, grants are still available to you to cover all or part of your travel costs overseas from other government departments.

An example of this is the aid available from the Training Agency. It is generally recognised that services such as travel, tourism and leisure related service activities will play an increasingly important part in our lives and in the economy.

To take full advantage of this trend and maximise the opportunities available, it is essential that the people involved in these activities are professionally trained.

A wide variety of courses attracting financial support is therefore available from the Training Agency. In many of these courses, travel to overseas leisure facilities for fact-finding is required, and the costs involved in this are either part or fully reimbursed by the Training Agency.

To obtain information on these courses, enquiries should be made to any Jobcentre or Training Agency Regional Office or alternatively information may be obtained from:
The Training Agency, Moorfoot, Sheffield, Yorks., S1 4PQ

Assistance From Other Bodies

The foregoing pages have been concerned with assistance from central government sources. In addition to these local sources of aid are also available. These sources exist within the local government area and can be classified under the following headings:
(a)   Educational and cultural assistance
(b)   Economic development

Educational and cultural assistance
For overseas study where a course requires study at an institution for at least one term, assistance may be given at the following rates by the Local Education Authority on a yearly basis (30 weeks & 3 days).

Highest cost countries £3,330 p.a. (Finland, Japan, Norway and the USA), additional weeks £83.35.

Higher cost countries £2,935 p.a. (Austria, Canada, Denmark, Eire, France, West Germany, Netherlands, Sweden and Switzerland), additional weeks £70.60.

High cost countries £2,545 p.a. (Belgium, Hong Kong, Italy, Indonesia and the USSR), additional weeks £57.80.

All other countries not mentioned above £2,155 p.a., additional weeks £45.05.

Overseas Conference Grants
Limited financial assistance towards travelling expenses is available from the British Academy. As a guideline, grants do not normally exceed the cost of the cheapest Apex-type fare, subject to a maximum of £650. Applications need to be made between three to six months, prior to the conference taking place.

In addition to conference assistance, the Academy administers a number of funds for overseas visits to the following areas:

Eastern Europe, China, USA, Japan, Switzerland, France, Spain, Latin America and Southeast Asia.

Further information and application forms may be obtained from: The British Academy, 20–21,Cornwall Terrace, London, NW1 4QP

ECONOMIC DEVELOPMENT

Apart from educational course assistance, there may well also be cultural links assistance available through the Local Authority having established a "town twinning" link with an overseas authority, broadly similar to itself in terms of population, or other characteristics etc. To find out about any town twinning link which exists and the types of exchanges made between the two parties, enquiries should be made to the Chief Executive's Department of the Local Authority area in which you are resident.

The other type of assistance available from Local Authority sources are those covering economic development at a local or regional level — district, county and regional. Enquiries should be made to the economic development department of the district council, county council or regional agency. A specialist body which specialises in information about Local Authority developments in this field is:

Centre for Local Economic Strategies Ltd., (CLES), Alberton House, St. Mary's Parsonage, Manchester, M3 2WJ Tel. 061-834 7036

COURIER SERVICES

In a world where the pursuit of business demands ever faster methods of communication, traditional services are too slow and electronic services may be unsuitable for security reasons. This is true for delivery of the following:

(1) High security or sensitive documents where confidentiality, originals or time are important.

(2) Samples of merchandise required urgently for fashion fairs, shows, etc.

(3) Clearance of large cheques drawn on distant banks e.g. within the United States this is a large-scale problem. If one considers the distance between New York and California then one can appreciate the difficulties involved.

(4) Delivery of documents or negotiable securities where the local postal system is unsafe (e.g. it is common practice for air tickets to be delivered by hand in Middle East countries because theft of them is widespread).

In these cases it can be seen that traditional methods of securing delivery such as post and freight are too slow and cumbersome and electronic methods are insecure or unsuitable. To service this particular market and overcome the drawbacks above, a new, rapidly growing service industry has emerged i.e. the air courier service. Using an air courier means that parcels can be moved as passenger baggage with the advantages of later check-in and quicker clearance than freight, giving a speedy, reliable desk-to-desk collection and delivery service for time sensitive documents and small parcels.

Obviously, air courier companies employ only a minimum number of full-time staff, since their service is "demand led" and required at very short notice.

Overcoming The Problem of Few Full-Time Staff

To maximise income and minimise fixed costs courier companies therefore use "independent contractors" to cope with peaks in demand. These are people who will act on the company's behalf, and who are prepared at very short notice to accompany the courier bags in flight.

What Does A Courier Do?

The courier is the passenger who accompanies the courier bags from airport to airport only. There are no collections or deliveries involved at either end. The courier travels with generally more than one package — small parcels are made up into large courier bags which are checked in on the courier's behalf by the company's ground staff.

Normally all the free baggage allowances are taken up by the courier bags with the result that only hand luggage allowances may be utilised by the courier but there are destinations where the courier does not have to release the check-in baggage allowance. With CTS (Courier Travel Services) baggage allowances have to be released at these destinations: New York (Concorde), Miami, Kuwait, Hong Kong (12-day trips), Johannesburg and *all* European destinations. This point should be checked out with the air courier company before finalising any arrangements. If the company utilises all the free baggage allowance *and* the hand luggage allowance is insufficient for the traveller's requirements *then* he or she will need to pay an additional baggage allowance. Whether this should be done depends on the amount of the charge for the additional baggage, which is governed by the destination; vis-à-vis the savings made on the courier ticket. The decision is yours to work out!

In respect of the vast bulk of destinations, should it be necessary to pay an additional baggage charge, this method of travel still offers substantial savings over any other. The courier bags are carried in the hold of the aircraft just like passenger suitcases and the courier only takes on board the manifests and paperwork required by customs at the other end.

How Does One Apply?

By contacting a courier company and arranging outward and return flights or going on a roster. Some courier companies have a highly organised system e.g. CTS (Courier Travel Services) which operate an on-board courier broker service for the major international courier companies and take bookings approximately three months in advance.

What Are The Requirements?

The general requirements for applicants are as below:

(a) Age 18–70 in good health and if pregnant a certificate of expected date of confinement is needed. Pregnancy over five months disallows the applicant.
(b) No criminal record in any country.
(c) Must be in possession of a valid Full Passport.

British and Irish Passport Holders may need visas for both the USA and Australia. Though the requirement of visas for the USA was abolished in 1988 this does not appear to have reached down yet to the lowest levels of US Immigration and Customs. However, the United States Immigration Service hope to solve this problem, by stationing immigration officers at the point of departure in the United Kingdom. This is being tried out at Heathrow Airport during the summer of 1990, and if successful, may become a permanent arrangement. For other countries visas may be required, depending on the company's operating practices, and on whether you need to pass through Immigration procedures — the courier company will advise on this point.

What About Insurance?

As a ticketed airline passenger you are protected against any damage caused while in the aircraft but normally you also need to take out separate travel insurance in respect of Personal Accident, Medical Expenses, etc.

What About Onward Travel to Other Destinations in the Country of Arrival?

The larger courier companies operate conjunction travel schemes with their travel agents to accommodate these extra requirements.

What are the Benefits?

The courier gets to fly free or at reduced rate on scheduled services and thus avoid the restrictions, inflexibility and delays associated with cheap charter and package flights. In an attempt to cope with the explosion in air travel and the strain that this imposes on inadequate air traffic handling control, the United Kingdom Civil Aviation Authority in 1988 imposed a scheme of priority and rationing on rescheduled flying slots, when the original flying slot had been missed. This policy has greatly favoured scheduled services with the result that less than 5% of scheduled services were delayed in departure time. On the other hand, charter and package flights have been delayed for up to 24 hours or longer in some cases.

This has important ramifications for travel insurance which now forms a substantial travel cost. With the use of scheduled services, the possibility of lengthy delay is very small with the result that delay cover on insurance is unnecessary, making travel insurance for scheduled services cheaper to obtain.

Specialist travel insurance to cover the minimal insurance requirements of couriers may be obtained through Wanderscan Ltd., 22, Parkside, Middleton, Lancs., M24 1NL, England.

Generation of Further Free and Reduced Rate Travel Allowances

The air courier method of travel offers an extremely cost effective method of reducing scheduled air travel costs for both business and leisure use for the independent traveller. The savings made are substantial in themselves, but can be made even more so by being tied into the special benefits schemes available on ticketing and regular air travel.

To maximise the benefits available this chapter should be read in conjunction with the chapters on "Ticketing" and "Bonus Travel".

Fare Comparisons, Destinations and Courier Companies

Sample fares and destinations are shown below. All the companies are members of AICES i.e. the Association of International Courier and Express Services.

The destinations listed are a sample only. Couriers are needed to fly to anywhere in the world, subject to demand and the current air courier network ex-London Heathrow comprises over 1,400 flying sectors, thereby ensuring that practically every destination in the world is available.

FARE COMPARISONS

All fares are return ex-Heathrow quoted in sterling.

Destination	Airline Courier	Fare £	Std. Fare £	Duration of stay days
PARIS	B/Airways	50	70–180	2
ROME	B/Airways	50	162–370	2–28
LISBON	B/Airways	80	119–306	2–28
VIENNA	B/Airways/ Austrian A/Lines	50	183–394	2–28
BASLE	B/Airways/	50	106–284	2–28
GENEVA	Swissair	50	ditto.	2–28
NEW YORK	B/Airways	200	230–892	2–28
	Concorde	410	2,460	2–28
CHICAGO	KLM	150	230–582	2–28
LOS ANGELES	B/Airways	250	322–770	2–28

Destination	Airline Courier	Fare £	Std. Fare £	Duration of stay days
S/FRANCISCO	B/Airways	250	ditto	2–28
HOUSTON	B/Airways	150	276–680	2–28
MIAMI	B/Airways	300	230–592	14 DAYS
DALLAS	B/Airways	150	276–794	2–28
TORONTO	B/Airways Air Canada	150	392–630	2–28
RIO	B/Airways	400	700–1,563	2–38
SYDNEY	Qantas/ Singapore Airlines	650	858–1,142	2–28
MELBOURNE	Qantas/ Air N. Zealand	650	966–1,142	2–28
HONG KONG	B/Airways Cathay Pacific	350	604–1,122	12 DAYS 2–28
SINGAPORE	Singapore Airlines/ B/Airways	350	518–1,094	14 DAYS
JO'BURG	B/Airways	500	561–962	2–28
HARARE	B/Airways	350	683–938	2–28
KUWAIT	B/Airways	250	438–942	14 DAYS

All fares shown are at March 1990 as supplied from CTS. Comparisons between courier fares and standard fares have been made on Class Y — Economy tickets. Conditions on these tickets vary, in terms of stay requirements, from those attaching to courier fares.

One-way flights to Australia and the USA are available.

For conjunction travel arrangements and flights originating in the USA telephone CTS Los Angeles Office 010-1-213 568 3381.

In respect of these and other destinations (mainly European) Quick International Couriers (UK) Ltd. supply free return tickets, and also pay any direct expenses involved.

To make a booking for the courier service flights contact the following:

Courier Travel Services Ltd., Johnson House, Browells Lane, Feltham, Middlesex, TW13 7EQ. Tel 01-844 2626 Telex 927501 Fax 01-844 2666

Quick International Couriers (UK) Ltd., Unit 18, Central Trading Estate, Staines Middlesex, TW18 4XE. Tel 0784-63431 Telex 8954916 QIC UK

A comprehensive list of air courier companies which belong to the relevant trade association may be obtained from the following:

Association of International Courier Express Services (AICES), P.O. Box 10, Leatherhead, Surrey, TW9 1SA Telephone 037-284 2953

It should be noted that AICES is a trade association which represents the interests of the air courier industry. It does *not* arrange courier flights.

USA: in addition to CTS mentioned above, courier flights can also be arranged through Now Voyager which charges a small registration fee. Telephone 010-1-212 431 1616.

SHARE PERKS

A development in recent years has been the proliferation of schemes giving benefits normally by way of discounts from companies to their shareholders. These are carried out for several reasons.

In the first place, it is an obvious development in many ways — after all, if people have been prepared to invest their money in the company's stock, then why not reward them with a discount off the product range of the company?

Secondly, the most usual reasons why people invest in the shares of a company are that they hope to see an appreciation of capital on those shares and to enjoy the dividend income relating to them. It may well be that the shareholder has never even used or bought the products or services forming the basis of the company's existence.

Thirdly, if the company is not seen as an attractive vehicle for investment a shareholder benefit scheme can be a means of attracting investors who share the aspirations and objectives of the company and regard capital appreciation and income growth motives as secondary to the ethical aspects of investment.

Finally, a benefit scheme is also a way of maintaining the loyalty of shareholders. The advantages of this to the company are that if shareholders keep their stake, the scale and related costs of their company secretarial departments in the maintenance of an up-to-date register are reduced through fewer share transfers taking place. If the benefit scheme is set at a low qualifying holding, then the stock of the company is so widely dispersed, that it becomes extremely difficult and expensive for a predator to try and launch a takeover bid. The downside to this is that the legal requirements of informing shareholders by way of annual reports, annual general meetings etc. make for an expensive process though there are moves afoot to reduce the amount of information required to be sent to shareholders, a move prompted by recent large-scale privatisations.

These are therefore some of the reasons why companies launch shareholder benefit schemes. It has to be stressed however that if one is considering investment in a company offering a benefit scheme, the benefit scheme should not be the sole reason for making the investment — the prospects of capital appreciation and dividend income, the market which the company is in, whether it is growing or diminishing, and the opportunities or threats arising from this assessment are all factors to be taken into account before investment takes place.

In assessing the value of the relevant benefit scheme, the value of discounts offered plus the dividend income applicable to the shareholding and costs of acquiring the qualifying amount of shares need all to be taken into account. This has not been done here because fluctuation in share prices would make such an analysis out of date extremely quickly and possibly mislead the inexperienced reader. A simple method of assessing the value of the benefit is given later in this section. Purchases of shares can be made through any stock-broker or bank. Lastly, it has to be said that shareholder benefit schemes can be withdrawn at any time and therefore a check should be made to ensure that the scheme is still in operation before any share purchase is made.

A list of the companies and contact points offering share schemes giving benefits on air and travel-related products follows.

Company/Secretary
CROSSAIR, 8058, Zurich Airport, Zurich, Switzerland
Flight vouchers denominated in Swiss francs (10 or 15) which are able to be used for payment of fares up to a maximum of 50% dependent on holding.

R. Crowther, Esq., BARR & WALLACE ARNOLD, 21, The Calls, Leeds, LS2 7ER
$7\frac{1}{2}$% discount off package holidays. Minimum holding 250 shares.

P. H. Prescott, Esq., CATTLE's (Holdings), Hattemprice Court, 38, Springfield Way, Analy, Hull, HU10 6RR
Special offers on Parkhill Travel. Variable requirements.

W.M.A. Carroll, Esq., DOMINION INTL. GROUP, 49, Parkside, Wimbledon, London, SW19 5NB
Six shareholders picked to visit any location of their choice where Dominion has interests, by annual draw. No minimum holding.

A. Speilberg, Esq., GREENALL WHITLEY, Wilderspool Brewery, Warrington, Lancs., WA4 6RH
10% off 1 Summer & 1 Winter holiday or airfare in Arrowsmith or Skyfare brochure ex-Manchester Airport only. Minimum holding 400 Ordinary shares.

Mrs. J. Thomas, Esq., LONDON W/END TELEVISION, South

Bank T.V. Centre, Kent House, Upper Ground, London, SE1 9LT
10% off brochure prices for Page & Moy, Cresta World Travel and Sunspot Travel for shareholder and family travelling together on the same holiday. No minimum holding.

C. Andrews, Esq., LADBROKE GROUP, Chancel House, Neasden Lane, London, NW10 2XE
10% off Ladbroke Holiday Villages and 25% off accommodation rates at Club In Villa Resort, Eilat, Israel and Los Zocos, Lanzarote.

LONHRO, Cheapside House, 138, Cheapside, London, EC2V 6BL
30% off Kuoni Travel bookings for Melville Hotel, Mauritius plus 20% off room rates at Princess Hotels International excluding November and December. Minimum holding 100 shares.

B.C. Bowers, Esq., THE RANK ORGANISATION, 6, Connaught Place, London, W2 2EZ
10% off brochure prices for OSL, Wings, Ellerman Sunflight or Freshfields holidays up to a maximum of £5,000 for shareholder and family. Minimum holding 500 shares.

TRAFALGAR HOUSE, 1, Berkeley Street, London, W1X 6NW
10% off most QE2 & Sagafjord World Cruises & related air connections plus 15% off Cunard Hotels in the Caribbean. Minimum holding 250 Ordinary shares.

Comparison of Benefits to Investment Costs & Return on Capital

The method below is designed to allow a comparison to be made between costs, dividends payable and maximum benefit available.

(a)   In cases where no minimum number of shares are required, take the cost of purchasing 100 shares since this will normally be the minimum transaction handled by a broker.

The total costs of purchase are the price of the shares plus the commission payable on the purchase.

(b)   Multiply the dividend per share by the number of shares held to obtain total dividend income.

(c)   Take the maximum benefit available on a purchase of £1,000 of the company's products or services if the level of purchase is variable. Where the maximum level of purchase is stated, this should be used pro rata to £1,000 to assess the maximum benefit available allowing a common basis to be established.

(d)   Add the total dividend income and maximum benefit available: (b) + (c).

(e)   Divide the total at (d) by (a) and express as a percentage to determine the return on investment. Compare this with the same calculation carried out on the other shares and most importantly with other forms of investment.

The assumption behind this method of calculation is that the shareholder avails himself of the benefit each year. If this is not the case then the calculation will give a misleading comparison when compared with other forms of investment.

Secondly, share benefit schemes can be withdrawn at any time and if shares have been purchased purely on the basis of the benefit scheme then withdrawal will considerably lessen the return on the investment. To take account of these variables it is suggested that the calculation is done again without taking account of the share benefit scheme and then make the comparison against other forms of investment. It may well be that the return on the share investment still looks attractive. However, the points made earlier in this section are repeated here. Purchase of shares purely because of a benefit scheme should never be contemplated under any circumstances, neither should it be the deciding factor in investment in shares.

Finally it has to be said that the benefit schemes looked at in this section are for illustrative purposes only. They should in no way be regarded as advice to invest or not invest in the shares of the companies mentioned.

FURTHERMORE

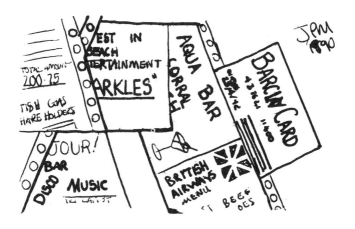

This section deals with miscellaneous aspects of travel mainly offering savings both in time and money to the traveller for personal and business travel under the following headings:

(a) Airline Passenger & Traveller Clubs
(b) No Subscription Holiday Clubs
(c) Your own discounted travel agency
(d) Business Travel Discounts
(e) Miscellaneous sources of reduced air travel

Airline Passenger & Traveller Clubs

Because of the inefficiency or unwillingness of travel agents to seek out the best value for the customer a number of the above clubs have come about to fill this demand. Membership of the clubs is normally by subscription and may be individual or corporate.

The services provided by clubs can be assessed by examining those offered by WEXAS International which is based in

London and offers both individual and corporate membership.

WEXAS CORPORATE GOLD MEMBERSHIP

(a) Discounted fares including First Class & Club discounts, ex-London, with free ticket delivery in central London.
(b) Telephone & telex booking.
(c) Discounts up to 25% on car rental.
(d) Global Hotel Discount programme up to 55% off with special rates and upgrades for central London.
(e) Worldwide year-round travel insurance at low rates and free flight accident insurance.
(f) Specialist route planning.

Additional benefits from membership may include bonus points on airline ticket purchase which may be used to obtain vouchers redeemable against further purchases — in effect fare reductions. This service is offered by IAPA Travel Services (International Airline Passengers Association).

CLUB CONTACT POINTS

WEXAS International, 45, Brompton Road, Knightsbridge, London, SW3 1DE Tel. 010-581 8767

IAPA, P.O. Box 113, London, SW1V 1ER Tel. 01-828 5841

No Subscription Holiday Clubs

These arise through members holding either Access or Barclaycard credit cards. The clubs offer discounts off both holidays and flights from selected operators if credit cards are used for the purchase. Discounts are made on a volume basis which approximate to 10% on purchases ranging from £200 (disc. £20) to £3,500+ (maximum disc. £250).

CONTACT POINTS

Access Holiday Club, Freepost, P.O. Box 44, Peterborough, PE1 1BR Tel. 0733-502714

Barclaycard Holiday Club, Page & Moy Ltd., P.O. Box 155, Leicester, LE2 1EH Tel. 0533-524455/524466

Your Own Discounted Travel Agency

This can be done in a variety of ways but whichever method is chosen, the essential thing to remember is that an ATOL (Air Travel Organiser's Licence) obtained direct, or alternatively using another operator's licence with his approval is first necessary. An ATOL licence is necessary before tickets can be sold to the general public.

Becoming an agent for an existing operator enables discounts to be obtained on personal travel and travel sold to the general public.

There are a number of variations on this. Some operate on a franchise basis, others as an agent off an existing licence and finally on a club basis using multi-level marketing.

FRANCHISE BASIS

EXCHANGE TRAVEL LTD., Exchange House, Parker Road, Hastings, East Sussex, TN34 3UB Tel. 0424-423571

This company operates a number of franchised outlets currently numbering about 100 nationwide. Basically, the franchise costs are a one-off payment of £7,500, plus 2% of turnover towards management expenses and marketing. Alternatively, for existing travel agents a conversion franchise at £3,000 is available. A buy-back option exists, where Exchange Travel will purchase the franchise for a minimum of 7.5% of the previous 12 months trading.

Discounted travel courses and agencies are available from: Skyline Travel, 407, The Strand, London, WC2 1ER Tel. 01-379 3364

Multi-level marketing
This operates through one becoming a member and introducing new members. Commission is given on both one's own bookings and those booked by the members introduced, averaging about 1–2% of total value. Schemes of this type are run by the following:

Time and Leisure International, Llanwye House, Hampton Park, Hereford, HR1 1XX Tel. 0432–269755

ATOL Licence enquiries should be addressed to:

Civil Aviation Authority, ATOL Section, 5th Floor, Tower Block, 45–59, Kingsway, London, WC2B 6NN Tel. 01–379 7311 Ext. 2687/2683

BUSINESS TRAVEL DISCOUNTS

These can be looked at in two ways, either by means of a volume discount on the amount of travel booked through the agent or on a frequently used route.

The size of discount which may be expected from placing all business through one agent on a volume commission basis will be normally as shown below, with slight variations.
£50,000 1%, £75,000 2%, £100,000+ 3%+

In addition to the normal commission received by agents on the sale of tickets, substantial additional commissions are paid to travel agents for directing customers to a particular route or carrier, where there are one or more competitors or routes.

This practice offers organisations the opportunity of boosting the commission rates mentioned overleaf, when frequent flights have to be made to a particular destination. In these circumstances, the client should insist on sharing the additional commission paid to the agent as a result of favouring a particular carrier or route.

If the volume of traffic and regularity of usage can be guaranteed an alternative method of handling this situation is to deal direct with the airline and forward book the seats, thus cutting out the agent *and* getting the standard agent commission of 9% on the bookings.

If the volume of business is sufficient then an implant arrangement could be considered. This is where the agent or airline provides a member of staff to the organisation to deal solely with travel bookings. Currently, expenditure of about £300,000 per annum would be necessary to make this arrangement viable.

Miscellaneous Sources of Reduced Air Travel

This category covers the acquisition of travel credits or opportunities from a number of sources:

Travel credits — UK
The Coupon People, 22, Chiltern Street, London, W1M 1PF 01-224 3919/3137
Bartered travel credits — USA
National Association of Trade Exchanges 010-1-617 828 3221

UK/USA

Free international advertising for these or anything else for that matter can be placed or read in the following free advertising paper, which circulates in both Manchester and London, and receives and exchanges advertising with similar free advertising, barter etc. papers overseas who are also members of FAPIA (Free Ads Papers International Association).

Loot, 26, Cross St., Manchester, M2 7AF 061-832 0099.

Travel related opportunities

Opportunities for these and areas connected to or complimentary with air travel e.g. import/export are advertised in an extremely useful UK mail-order publication called *Business Opportunities Directory* published by Prestige Publishing International, (Agy. 241), P.O. Box 783, Poole, Dorset, BH14 8YH

If you have any information, suggestions etc. on the subject of air travel which you would like to see included in future editions of this guide, please send them for consideration to Tynron Press, Stenhouse, Thornhill, Dumfriesshire DG3 4LD. Any material received and subsequently used will be acknowledged in the text . . . So get your pen and paper out, and get your name in print!